Charis Class

D1552817

The Changed Life

The Changed Life
By Henry Drummond

Wilder Publications, LLC.
PO Box 3005
Radford VA 24143-3005

ISBN 10: 1-60459-177-3
ISBN 13: 978-1-60459-177-4

First Edition

10 9 8 7 6 5 4 3 2 1

We All

With unveiled face

Reflecting

As a Mirror

The Glory of the Lord

Are transformed

Into the same image

From Glory to Glory

Even as from the Lord

The Spirit

Table of Contents

The Changed Life

"I protest that if some great power would agree to make me always think what is true and do what is right, on condition of being turned into a sort of clock and wound up every morning, I should instantly close with the offer."

These are the words of Mr. Huxley. The infinite desirability, the infinite difficulty of being good—the theme is as old as humanity. The man does not live from whose deeper being the same confession has not risen, or who would not give his all tomorrow, if he could "close with the offer" of becoming a better man.

I propose to make that offer now. In all seriousness, without being "turned into a sort of clock," the end can be attained. Under the right conditions it is as natural for character to become beautiful as for a flower; and if on God's earth, there is not some machinery for effecting it, the supreme gift to the world has been forgotten. This is simply what man was made for. With Browning: "I say that

Man was made to grow, not stop." Or in the deeper words of an older Book: "Whom He did foreknow, He also did predestinate . . . to be conformed to the Image of his Son."

Let me begin by naming, and in part discarding, some processes in vogue already, for producing better lives. These processes are far from wrong; in their place they may even be essential. One ventures to disparage them only because they do not turn out the most perfect possible work.

The first imperfect method is to rely on Resolution. In will-power, in mere spasms of earnestness there is no salvation. Struggle, effort, even agony, have their place in Christianity as we shall see; but this is not where they come in. In mid-Atlantic the other day, the Etruria in which I was sailing, suddenly stopped. Something had gone wrong with the engines. There were five hundred able-bodied men on board the ship. Do you think if we had gathered together and pushed against the masts we could have pushed it on? When one attempts to sanctify himself by effort, he is trying to make his boat go by pushing against the mast. He is like a drowning man trying to lift himself out of the water by pulling at the hair of his own head. Christ held up this method almost to ridicule when He said, "Which of you by taking thought can add a cubit to his stature?" The one redeeming feature of the self-sufficient method is this—that those who try it find out almost at once that it will not gain the goal.

Another experimenter says:—"But that is not my method. I have seen the folly of a mere wild struggle in the dark. I work on a principle. My plan is not to waste power on random effort, but to concentrate on a single sin. By taking one at a time and crucifying it steadily, I hope in the end to extirpate all." To this, unfortunately, there are four objections. For one thing life is too short; the name of sin is Legion. For another thing, to deal with individual sins is to leave the rest of the nature for the time untouched. In the third place, a single combat with a special sin does not affect the root and spring of the disease. If one only of the channels of sin be obstructed, experience points to an almost certain overflow through some other part of the nature. Partial conversion is almost always accompanied by such moral leakage, for the pent-up energies accumulate to the bursting point, and the last state of that soul may be worse than the first. In the last place, religion does not consist in negatives, in stopping this sin and stopping that. The perfect character can never be produced with a pruning knife.

But a Third protests:— "So be it I make no attempt to stop sins one by one. My method is just the opposite. I copy the virtues one by one." The difficulty about the copying method is that it is apt to be mechanical. One can always tell an engraving from a picture, an artificial flower from a real flower. To copy virtues one by one has somewhat the same effect as eradicating the vices one by one; the temporary result is an overbalanced and incongruous character. Someone defines a prig as "a creature that is over-fed for its size." One sometimes finds Christians of this species— over-fed on one side of their nature, but dismally thin and starved-looking on the other. The result, for instance, of copying Humility, and adding it on to an otherwise worldly life, is simply grotesque. A rabid Temperance advocate, for the same reason, is often the poorest of creatures, flourishing on a single virtue, and quite oblivious that his Temperance is making a worse man of him and not a better. These are examples of fine virtues spoiled by association with mean companions. Character is a unity, and all the virtues must advance together to make the perfect man. This method of sanctification, nevertheless, is in the true direction. It is only in the details of execution that it fails.

A fourth method I need scarcely mention, for it is a variation on those already named. It is the very young man's method; and the pure earnestness of it makes it almost desecration to touch it. It is to keep a private note-book with columns for the days of the week, and a list of virtues with spaces against each for marks. This, with many stern rules for preface, is stored away in a secret place, and from time to time, at nightfall, the soul is arraigned before it as before a private judgment bar. This living by code was Franklin's method; and I suppose thousands more could tell how they had hung up in their bed-rooms, or hid in lock-fast drawers, the rules which one solemn day they drew up to shape their lives. This method is not erroneous, only somehow its success is poor. You bear me witness that it fails? And it fails generally for very matter-of-fact reasons—most likely because one day we forget the rules.

All these methods that have been named —the self-sufficient method, the self-crucifixion method, the mimetic method, and the diary method—are perfectly human, perfectly natural, perfectly ignorant, and, as they stand, perfectly inadequate. It is not argued, I repeat, that they must be abandoned. Their harm is rather that they distract attention from the true working method, and secure a fair result at the expense of the perfect one. What that perfect method is we shall now go on to ask.

The Formula of Sanctification

A Formula, a receipt, for Sanctification— can one seriously speak of this mighty change as if the process were as definite as for the production of so many volts of electricity? It is impossible to doubt it. Shall a mechanical experiment succeed infallibly, and the one vital experiment of humanity remain a chance? Is corn to grow by method, and character by caprice? If we cannot calculate to a certainty that the forces of religion will do their work, then is religion vain. And if we cannot express the law of these forces in simple words, then is Christianity not the world's religion but the world's conundrum.

Where, then, shall one look for such a formula? Where one would look for any formula—among the text books. And if we turn to the text books of Christianity we shall find a formula for this problem as clear and precise as any in the mechanical sciences. If this simple rule, moreover, be but followed fearlessly, it will yield the result of a perfect character as surely as any result that is guaranteed by the laws of nature. The finest expression of this rule in Scripture, or indeed in any literature, is probably one drawn up and condensed into a single verse by Paul. You will find it in a letter—the second to the Corinthians—written by him to some Christian people who, in a city which was a byword for depravity and licentiousness, were seeking the higher life. To see the point of the words we must take them from the immensely improved rendering of the Revised translation, for the older Version in this case greatly obscures the sense. They are these: "We all, with unveiled face reflecting as a mirror the glory of the Lord, are transformed into the same image from glory to glory, even as from the Lord the Spirit."

Now observe at the outset the entire contradiction of all our previous efforts, in the simple passive "we are transformed." We are changed, as the Old Version has it—we do not change ourselves. No man can change himself. Throughout the New Testament you will find that wherever these moral and spiritual transformations are described the verbs are in the passive. Presently it will be pointed out that there is a rationale in this; but meantime do not toss these words aside as if this passivity denied all human effort or ignored intelligible law. What is implied for the soul here is no more than is everywhere claimed for the body. In physiology the verbs describing the processes of growth are in the passive. Growth is not voluntary; it takes place, it happens, it is wrought upon matter. So here. "Ye must be born again" —we cannot born ourselves. "Be not conformed to this world but be ye transformed"—we are subjects to a transforming influence, we do not transform ourselves. Not more certain is it that it is something outside the thermometer that produces a change in the thermometer, than it is something outside the soul of man that produces a moral change upon him. That he must be susceptible to that change, that he must be a party to it, goes without saying; but that neither his aptitude nor his will can produce it, is equally certain.

Obvious as it ought to seem, this may be to some an almost startling revelation. The change we have been striving after is not to be produced by any more striving after. It is to be wrought upon us by the moulding of hands beyond our own. As the branch ascends, and the bud bursts, and the fruit reddens under the co-operation of influences from the outside air, so man rises to the higher stature under invisible pressures from without. The radical defect of all our former methods of sanctification was the attempt to generate from within that which can only be wrought upon us from without. According to the first Law of Motion: Every body continues in its state of rest, or of uniform motion in a straight line, except in so far as it may be compelled by impressed forces to change that state. This is also a first law of Christianity. Every man's character remains as it is, or continues in the direction in which it is going, until it is compelled by impressed forces to change that state. Our failure has been the failure to put ourselves in the way of the impressed forces. There

is a clay, and there is a Potter; we have tried to get
the clay to mould the clay.

Whence, then, these pressures, and where this
Potter? The answer of the formula is "By reflecting
as a mirror the glory of the Lord we are changed."
But this is not very clear. What is the "glory" of the
Lord, and how can mortal man reflect it, and how
can that act as an "impressed force" in moulding him
to a nobler form? The word "glory" —the word which
has to bear the weight of holding those "impressed
forces" —is a stranger in current speech, and our
first duty is to seek out its equivalent in working
English. It suggests at first a radiance of some kind,
something dazzling or glittering, some halo such as
the old masters loved to paint round the heads of
their Ecce Homos. But that is paint, mere matter,
the visible symbol of some unseen thing. What is
that unseen thing? It is that of all unseen things, the
most radiant, the most beautiful, the most Divine,
and that is Character. On earth, in Heaven, there is
nothing so great, so glorious as this. The word has
many meanings; in ethics it can have but one. Glory
is character and nothing less, and it can be nothing
more. The earth is "full of the Glory of the Lord,"
because it is full of His character. The "Beauty of the
Lord" is character. "The effulgence of His Glory" is
character. "The Glory of the Only Begotten" is
character, the character which is "fulness of grace
and truth." And when God told His people His name
He simply gave them His character, His character
which was Himself. "And the Lord proclaimed the
Name of the Lord . . . the Lord, the Lord God,

merciful and gracious, long-suffering and abundant in goodness and truth." Glory then is not something intangible, or ghostly, or transcendental. If it were this, how could Paul ask men to reflect it? Stripped of its physical enswathement it is Beauty, moral and spiritual Beauty, Beauty infinitely real, infinitely exalted, yet infinitely near and infinitely communicable.

With this explanation read over the sentence once more in paraphrase: We all reflecting as a mirror the character of Christ are transformed into the same Image from character to character—from a poor character to a better one, from a better one to ane a little better still, from that to one still more complete, until by slow degrees the Perfect Image is attained. Here the solution of the problem of sanctification is compressed into a sentence: Reflect the character of Christ and you will become like Christ.

All men are mirrors—that is the first law on which this formula is based. One of the aptest descriptions of a human being is that he is a mirror. As we sat at table to-night, the world in which each of us lived and moved throughout this day was focussed in the room. What we saw as we looked at one another was not one another, but one mother's world. We were an arrangement of mirrors. The scenes we saw were all reproduced; the people we met walked to and fro; they spoke, they bowed, they passed us by, did everything over again as if it had been real. When we talked, we were but looking at our own mirror and describing what flitted across it; our listening was not hearing, but seeing—we but looked on our neighbour's mirror. All human intercourse is a seeing of reflections. I meet a stranger in a railway carriage. The cadence of his first word tells me he is English, and comes from Yorkshire. Without knowing it he has reflected his birthplace, his parents, and the long history of their race. Even physiologically he is a mirror. His second sentence records that he is a politician, and a faint inflexion in the way he pronounces The Times reveals his party. In his next remarks I see reflected a whole world of experiences. The books he has read, the people he has met, the influences that have played upon him and made him the man he is— these are all registered there by a pen which lets nothing pass, and whose writing can never be blotted out. What I am reading in him meantime he also is reading in me; and before the journey is over we could half write each other's lives. Whether we like it or not, we live in glass houses. The mind, the memory, the soul, is simply a vast chamber panelled with looking-glass. And upon this miraculous arrangement and endowment depends the capacity of mortal souls to "reflect the character of the Lord."

But this is not all. If all these varied reflections from our so-called secret life are patent to the world, how close the writing, how complete the record, within the soul itself? For the influences we meet are not simply held for a moment on the polished surface and thrown off again into space. Each is retained where first it fell, and stored up in the soul for ever.

This law of Assimilation is the second, and by far the most impressive truth which underlies the formula of sanctification—the truth that men are not only mirrors, but that these mirrors so far from being mere reflectors of the fleeting things they see, transfer into their own inmost substance, and hold in permanent preservation the things that they reflect. No one knows how the soul can hold these things. No one knows how the miracle is done. No phenomenon in nature, no process in chemistry, no chapter in necromancy can even help us to begin to understand this amazing operation. For, think of it, the past is not only focussed there, in a man's soul, it is there. How could it be reflected from there if it were not there? All things that he has ever seen, known, felt, believed of the surrounding world are now within him, have become part of him, in part are him—he has been changed into their image. He may deny it, he may resent it, but they are there. They do not adhere to him, they are transfused through him. He cannot alter or rub them out. They are not in his memory, they are in him. His soul is as they have filled it, made it, left it. These things, these books, these events, these influences are his makers. In their hands are life and death, beauty and deformity. When once the image or likeness of any of these is fairly presented to the soul, no power on earth can hinder two things happening—it must be absorbed into the soul, and for ever reflected back again from character.

Upon these astounding yet perfectly obvious psychological facts, Paul bases his doctrine of sanctification. He sees that character is a thing built up by slow degrees, that it is hourly changing for better or for worse according to the images which flit across it. One step further and the whole length and breadth of the application of these ideas to the central problem of religion will stand before us.

The Alchemy of Influence

If events change men, much more persons. No man can meet another on the street without making some mark upon him. We say we exchange words when we meet; what we exchange is souls. And when intercourse is very close and very frequent, so complete is this exchange that recognisable bits of the one soul begin to show in the other's nature, and the second is conscious of a similar and growing debt to the first. This mysterious approximating of two souls who has not witnessed? Who has not watched some old couple come down life's pilgrimage hand in hand with such gentle trust and joy in one another that their very faces wore the self-same look? These were not two souls; it was a composite soul. It did not matter to which of the two you spoke, you would have said the same words to either. It was quite indifferent which replied, each would have said the same. Half a century's reflecting had told upon them: they were changed into the same image. It is the Law of Influence that we become like those whom we habitually admire: these had become like because they habitually admired. Through all the range of literature, of history, and biography this law presides. Men are all mosaics of other men. There was a savour of David about Jonathan and a savour of Jonathan about David. Jean Valjean, in the masterpiece of Victor Hugo, is Bishop Bienvenu risen from the dead. Metempsychosis is a fact. George Eliot's message to the world was that men and women make men and women. The Family, the cradle of mankind, has no meaning apart from this. Society itself is nothing but a rallying point for these omnipotent forces to do their work. On the doctrine of Influence, in short, the whole vast pyramid of humanity is built.

But it was reserved for Paul to make the supreme application of the Law of Influence. It was a tremendous inference to make, but he never hesitated. He himself was a changed man: he knew exactly what had done it; it was Christ On the Damascus road they met, and from that hour his life was absorbed in His. The effect could not but follow—on words, on deeds, on career, on creed. The "impressed forces" did their vital work. He became like Him whom he habitually loved. "So we all," he writes, "reflecting as a mirror the glory of Christ are changed into the same image."

Nothing could be more simple, more intelligible, more natural, more supernatural. It is an analogy from an everyday fact Since we are what we are by the impacts of those who surround us, those who surround themselves with the highest will be those who change into the highest. There are some men and some women in whose company we are always at our best. While with them we cannot think mean thoughts or speak ungenerous words. Their mere presence is elevation, purification, sanctity. All the best stops in our nature are drawn out by their intercourse, and we find a music in our souls that was never there before. Suppose even that influence prolonged through a month, a year, a lifetime, and what could not life become? Here, even on the common plane of life, talking our language, walking our streets, working side by side, are sanctifiers of souls; here, breathing through common play, is Heaven; here, energies charged even through a temporal medium with a virtue of regeneration. If to live with men, diluted to the millionth degree with the virtue of the Highest, can exalt and purify the nature, what bounds can be set to the influence of Christ? To live with Socrates—with unveiled face—must have made one wise; with Aristides, just. Francis of Assisi must have made one gentle; Savonarola, strong. But to have lived with Christ? To have lived with Christ must have made one like Christ; that is to say, A Christian.

As a matter of fact, to live with Christ did produce this effect. It produced it in the case of Paul. And during Christ's lifetime the experiment was tried in an even more startling form. A few raw, unspiritual, uninspiring men, were admitted to the inner circle of His friendship. The change began at once. Day by day we can almost see the first disciples grow. First there steals over them the faintest possible adumbration of His character, and occasionally, very occasionally, they do a thing, or say a thing that they could not have done or said had they not been living there. Slowly the spell of His Life deepens. Reach after reach of their nature is overtaken, thawed, subjugated, sanctified. Their manners soften, their words become more gentle, their conduct more unselfish As swallows who have found a summer, as frozen buds the spring, their starved humanity bursts into a fuller life. They do not know how it is, but they are different men. One day they find themselves like their Master, going about and doing good. To themselves it is unaccountable, but they cannot do otherwise. They were not told to do it, it came to them to do it. But the people who watch them know well how to account for it—"They have been," they whisper, "with Jesus." Already even, the mark and seal of His character is upon them— "They have been with Jesus." Unparalleled phenomenon, that these poor fishermen should remind other men of Christ! Stupendous victory and mystery of regeneration that mortal men should suggest to the world, God!

There is something almost melting in the way His contemporaries, and John especially, speak of the Influence of Christ. John lived himself in daily wonder at Him; he was overpowered, overawed, entranced, transfigured. To his mind it was impossible for any one to come under this influence and ever be the same again. "Whosoever abideth in Him sinneth not," he said. It was inconceivable that he should sin, as inconceivable as that ice should live in a burning sun, or darkness co-exist with noon.

If any one did sin, it was to John the simple proof that he could never have met Christ. "Whosoever sinneth," he exclaims, "hath not seen Him, neither known Him." Sin was abashed in this Presence. Its roots withered. Its sway and victory were for ever at an end.

But these were His contemporaries. It was easy for them to be influenced by Him, for they were every day and all the day together. But how can we mirror that which we have never seen? How can all this stupendous result be produced by a Memory, by the scantiest of all Biographies, by One who lived and left this earth eighteen hundred years ago? How can modern men to-day make Christ, the absent Christ, their most constant companion still? The answer is that Friendship is a spiritual thing. It is independent of Matter, or Space, or Time. That which I love in my friend is not that which I see. What influences me in my friend is not his body but his spirit. It would have been an ineffable experience truly to have lived at that time—

"I think when I read the sweet story of old,
How when Jesus was here among men,
He took little children like lambs to His fold,
I should like to have been with him then.

"I wish that His hand had been laid on my head,
That His arms had been thrown around me,
And that I had seen His kind look when He said,
Let the little ones come unto Me."

And yet, if Christ were to come into the world again few of us probably would ever have a chance of seeing Him. Millions of her subjects, in this little country, have never seen their own Queen. And there would be millions of the subjects of Christ who could never get within speaking distance of Him if He were here. Our companionship with Him, like all true companionship, is a spiritual communion. All friendship, all love, human and Divine, is purely spiritual. It was after He was risen that He influenced even the disciples most. Hence in reflecting the character of Christ it is no real obstacle that we may never have been in visible contact with Himself.

There lived once a young girl whose perfect grace of character was the wonder of those who knew her. She wore on her neck a gold locket which no one was ever allowed to open. One day, in a moment of unusual confidence, one of her companions was allowed to touch its spring and learn its secret. She saw written these words— "Whom having not seen, I love." That was the secret of her beautiful life. She had been changed into the Same Image.

Now this is not imitation, but a much deeper thing. Mark this distinction. For the difference in the process, as well as in the result, may be as great as that between a photograph secured by the infallible pencil of the sun, and the rude outline from a schoolboy's chalk. Imitation is mechanical, reflection organic. The one is occasional, the other habitual. In the one case, man comes to God and imitates Him; in the other, God comes to man and imprints Himself upon him. It is quite true that there is an imitation of Christ which amounts to reflection. But Paul's term includes all that the other holds, and is open to no mistake.

"Make Christ your most constant companion"—this is what it practically means for us. Be more under His influence than under any other influence. Ten minutes spent in His society every day, ay, two minutes if it be face to face, and heart to heart, will make the whole day different. Every character has an inward spring, let Christ be it. Every action has a key-note, let Christ set it. Yesterday you got a certain letter. You sat down and wrote a reply which almost scorched the paper. You picked the cruellest adjectives you knew and sent it forth, without a pang, to do its ruthless work. You did that because your life was set in the wrong key. You began the day with the mirror placed at the wrong angle. To-morrow, at daybreak, turn it towards Him, and even to your enemy the fashion of your countenance will be changed. Whatever you then do, one thing you will find you could not do—you could not write that letter. Your first impulse may be the same, your judgment may be unchanged, but if you try it the ink will dry on your pen, and you will rise from your desk an unavenged but a greater and more Christian man. Throughout the whole day your actions, down to the last detail, will do homage to that early vision. Yesterday you thought mostly about yourself. To-day the poor will meet you, and you will feed them. The helpless, the tempted, the sad, will throng about you, and each you will befriend. Where were all these people yesterday? Where they are to-day, but you did not see them. It is in reflected light that the poor are seen. But your soul to-day is not at the ordinary angle. "Things which are not seen" are visible. For a few short hours you live the Eternal Life. The eternal life, the life of faith, is simply the life of the higher vision. Faith is an attitude— a mirror set at the right angle.

When to-morrow is over, and in the evening you review it, you will wonder how you did it. You will not be conscious that you strove for anything, or imitated anything, or crucified anything. You will be conscious of Christ; that He was with you, that without compulsion you were yet compelled, that without force, or noise, or proclamation, the revolution was accomplished. You do not congratulate yourself as one who has done a mighty deed, or achieved a personal success, or stored up a fund of "Christian experience" to ensure the same result again. What you are conscious of is "the glory of the Lord." And what the world is conscious of, if the result be a true one, is also "the glory of the Lord." In looking at a mirror one does not see the mirror, or think of it, but only of what it reflects. For a mirror never calls attention to itself except when there are flaws in it.

That this is a real experience and not a vision, that this life is possible to men, is being lived by men to-day, is simple biographical fact. From a thousand witnesses I cannot forbear to summon one. The following are the words of one of the highest intellects this age has known, a man who shared the burdens of his country as few have done, and who, not in the shadows of old age, but in the high noon of his success, gave this confession—I quote it with only a few abridgments—to the world:—

`I want to speak to-night only a little, but that little I desire to speak of the sacred name of Christ, who is my life, my inspiration, my hope, and my surety. I cannot help stopping and looking back upon the past. And I wish, as if I had never done it before, to bear witness, not only that it is by the grace of God, but that it is by the grace of God as manifested in Christ Jesus, that I am what I am. I recognize the sublimity and grandeur of the revelation of God in His eternal fatherhood as one that made the heavens, that founded the earth, and that regards all the tribes of the earth, comprehending them in one universal mercy; but it is the God that is manifested in Jesus Christ, revealed by His life, made known by the inflections of His feelings, by His discourse, and by His deeds—it is that God that I desire to confess to-night, and of whom I desire to say, "By the love of God in Christ Jesus I am what I am."

`If you ask me precisely what I mean by that, I say, frankly, that more than any recognized influence of my father or my mother upon me; more than the social influence of all the members of my father's household; more, so far as I can trace it, or so far as I am made aware of it, than all the social influences of every kind, Christ has had the formation of my mind and my disposition. My hidden ideals of what is beautiful I have drawn from Christ. My thoughts of what is manly, and noble, and pure, have almost all of them arisen from the Lord Jesus Christ. Many men have educated themselves by reading Plutarch's Lives of the Ancient Worthies, and setting before themselves one and another of these that in different ages have achieved celebrity; and they have recognized the great power of these men on themselves. Now I do not perceive that poet, or philosopher, or reformer, or general, or any other great man, ever has dwelt in my imagination and in my thought as the simple Jesus has. For more than twenty-five years I instinctively have gone to Christ to draw a measure and a rule for everything. Whenever there has been a necessity for it, I have sought—and at last almost spontaneously—to throw myself into the companionship of Christ; and early, by my imagination, I could see Him standing and looking quietly and lovingly upon me. There seemed almost to drop from His face an influence upon me that suggested what was the right thing in the controlling of passion, in the subduing of pride, in the overcoming of selfishness; and it is from Christ, manifested to my inward eye, that I have consciously derived more ideals, more models, more influences, than from any human character whatever.

`That is not all. I feel conscious that I have derived from the Lord Jesus Christ every thought that makes heaven a reality to me, and every thought that paves the road that lies between me and heaven. All my conceptions of the progress of grace in the soul; all the steps by which divine life is

evolved; all the ideals that overhang the blessed
sphere which awaits us beyond this world —these
are derived from the Saviour. The life that I now live
in the flesh I live by the faith of the Son of God.

`That is not all. Much as my future includes all
these elements which go to make the blessed fabric
of earthly life, yet, after all, what the summer is
compared with all its earthly products —flowers, and
leaves, and grass—that is Christ compared with all
the products of Christ in my mind and in my soul.
All the flowers and leaves of sympathy; all the
twining joys that come from my heart as a
Christian—these I take and hold in the future, but
they are to me what the flowers and leaves of
summer are compared with the sun that makes the
summer. Christ is the Alpha and Omega, the
beginning and the end of my better life.

`When I read the Bible, I gather a great deal from
the Old Testament, and from the Pauline portions of
the New Testament; but after all, I am conscious
that the fruit of the Bible is Christ. That is what I
read it for, and that is what I find that is worth
reading. I have had a hunger to be loved of Christ.
You all know, in some relations, what it is to be
hungry for love. Your heart seems unsatisfied till
you can draw something more toward you from those
that are dearest to you. There have been times when
I have had an unspeakable heart-hunger for Christ's
love. My sense of sin is never strong when I think of
the law; my sense of sin is strong when I think of
love—if there is any difference between law and
love. It is when drawing near the Lord Jesus Christ,

and longing to be loved, that I have the most vivid sense of unsymmetry, of imperfection, of absolute unworthiness, and of my sinfulness. Character and conduct are never so vividly set before me as when in silence I bend in the presence of Christ, revealed not in wrath, but in love to me. I never so much long to be lovely, that I may be loved, as when I have this revelation of Christ before my mind.

`In looking back upon my experience, that part of my life which stands out, and which I remember most vividly, is just that part that has had some conscious association with Christ. All the rest is pale, and thin, and lies like clouds on the horizon. Doctrines, systems, measures, methods— what may be called the necessary mechanical and external part of worship; the part which the senses would recognize—this seems to have withered and fallen off like leaves of last summer; but that part which has taken hold of Christ abides'

Can anyone hear this life-music, with its throbbing refrain of Christ, and remain unmoved by envy or desire? Yet till we have lived like this we have never lived at all.

The First Experiment

Then you reduce religion to a common Friendship? A common Friendship—Who talks of a common Friendship? There is no such thing in the world. On earth no word is more sublime. Friendship is the nearest thing we know to what religion is. God is love. And to make religion akin to Friendship is simply to give it the highest expression conceivable by man. But if by demurring to "a common friendship" is meant a protest against the greatest and the holiest in religion being spoken of in intelligible terms, then I am afraid the objection is all too real. Men always look for a mystery when one talks of sanctification; some mystery apart from that which must ever be mysterious wherever Spirit works. It is thought some peculiar secret lies behind it, some occult experience which only the initiated know. Thousands of persons go to church every Sunday hoping to solve this mystery. At meetings, at conferences, many a time they have reached what they thought was the very brink of it, but somehow no further revelation came. Poring over religious books, how often were they not within a paragraph of it; the next page, the next sentence, would discover all, and they would be borne on a flowing tide for ever. But nothing happened. The next sentence and the next page were read, and still it eluded them; and though the promise of its coming kept faithfully up to the end, the last chapter found them still pursuing. Why did nothing happen? Because there was nothing to happen—nothing of the kind they were looking for. Why did it elude them? Because there was no "it" When shall we learn that the pursuit of holiness is simply the pursuit of Christ? When shall we substitute for the "it" of a fictitious aspiration, the approach to a Living Friend? Sanctity is in character and not in moods; Divinity in our own plain calm humanity, and in no mystic rapture of the soul.

And yet there are others who, for exactly a contrary reason, will find scant satisfaction here. Their complaint is not that a religion expressed in terms of Friendship is too homely, but that it is still too mystical. To "abide" in Christ, to "make Christ our most constant companion" is to them the purest mysticism. They want something absolutely tangible and absolutely direct. These are not the poetical souls who seek a sign, a mysticism in excess; but the prosaic natures whose want is mathematical definition in details. Yet it is perhaps not possible to reduce this problem to much more rigid elements. The beauty of Friendship is its infinity, One can never evacuate life of mysticism. Home is full of it, love is full of it, religion is full of it. Why stumble at that in the relation of man to Christ which is natural in the relation of man to man?

If any one cannot conceive or realize a mystical relation with Christ, perhaps all that can be done is to help him to step on to it by still plainer analogies from common life. How do I know Shakespeare or Dante? By communing with their words and thoughts. Many men know Dante better than their own fathers. He influences them more. As a spiritual presence he is more near to them, as a spiritual force more real. Is there any reason why a greater than Shakespeare or Dante, who also walked this earth, who left great words behind Him, who has great works everywhere in the world now, should not also instruct, inspire, and mould the characters of men? I do not limit Christ's influence to this. It is this, and it is more. But Christ, so far from resenting or discouraging this relation of Friendship, Himself proposed it. "Abide in Me" was almost His last word to the world. And He partly met the difficulty of those who feel its intangibleness by adding the practical clause, "If ye abide in Me and My words abide in you."

Begin with His words. Words can scarcely ever be long impersonal. Christ Himself was a Word, a word made Flesh. Make His words flesh; do them, live them, and you must live Christ. "He that keepeth My commandments, he it is that loveth Me." Obey Him and you must love Him. Abide in Him and you must obey Him. Cultivate His Friendship. Live after Christ, in His Spirit, as in His Presence, and it is difficult to think what more you can do. Take this at

least as a first lesson, as introduction. If you cannot
at once and always feel the play of His life upon
yours, watch for it also indirectly. "The whole earth
is full of the character of the Lord." Christ is the
Light of the world, and much of His Light is reflected
from things in the world—even from clouds. Sunlight
is stored in every leaf, from leaf through coal, and it
comforts us thence when days are dark and we
cannot see the sun. Christ shines through men,
through books, through history, through nature,
music, art. Look for Him there. "Every day one
should either look at a beautiful picture, or hear
beautiful music, or read a beautiful poem." The real
danger of mysticism is not making it broad enough.

Do not think that nothing is happening because
you do not see yourself grow, or hear the whirr of the
machinery. All great things grow noiselessly. You
can see a mushroom grow, but never a child. Mr.
Darwin tells us that Evolution proceeds by
"numerous, successive, and slight modifications."
Paul knew that, and put it, only in more beautiful
words, into the heart of his formula. He said for the
comforting of all slowly perfecting souls that they
grew "'from character to character." "The inward
man" he says elsewhere, "is renewed from day to
day." All thorough work is slow; all true
development by minute slight and insensible
metamorphoses. The higher the structure, moreover,
the slower the progress. As the biologist runs his eye
over the long Ascent of Life he sees the lowest forms
of animals develop in an hour; the next above these
reach maturity in a day; those higher still take

weeks or months to perfect; but the few at the top demand the long experiment of years. If a child and an ape are born on the same day the last will be in full possession of its faculties and doing the active work of life before the child has left its cradle. Life is the cradle of eternity. As the man is to the animal in the slowness of his evolution, so is the spiritual man to the natural man. Foundations which have to bear the weight of an eternal life must be surely laid. Character is to wear for ever; who will wonder or grudge that it cannot be developed in a day?

To await the growing of a soul, nevertheless, is an almost Divine act of faith. How pardonable, surely, the impatience of deformity with itself, of a consciously despicable character standing before Christ, wondering, yearning, hungering to be like that? Yet must one trust the process fearlessly, and without misgiving. "The Lord the Spirit" will do His part. The tempting expedient is, in haste for abrupt or visible progress, to try some method less spiritual, or to defeat the end by watching for effects instead of keeping the eye on the Cause. A photograph prints from the negative only while exposed to the sun. While the artist is looking to see how it is getting on he simply stops the getting on. Whatever of wise supervision the soul may need, it is certain it can never be over-exposed, or, that, being exposed, anything else in the world can improve the result or quicken it. The creation of a new heart, the renewing of a right spirit is an omnipotent work of God. Leave it to the Creator. "He which hath begun a good work in you will perfect it unto that day."

No man, nevertheless, who feels the worth and solemnity of what is at stake will be careless as to his progress. To become like Christ is the only thing in the world worth caring for, the thing before which every ambition of man is folly, and all lower achievement vain. Those only who make this quest the supreme desire and passion of their lives can even begin to hope to reach it. If, therefore, it has seemed up to this point as if all depended on passivity, let me now assert, with conviction more intense, that all depends on activity. A religion of effortless adoration may be a religion for an angel but never for a man. Not in the contemplative, but in the active lies true hope; not in rapture, but in reality lies true life; not in the realm of ideals but among tangible things is man's sanctification wrought. Resolution, effort, pain, self-crucifixion, agony—all the things already dismissed as futile in themselves must now be restored to office, and a tenfold responsibility laid upon them. For what is their office? Nothing less than to move the vast inertia of the soul, and place it, and keep it where the spiritual forces will act upon it. It is to rally the forces of the will, and keep the surface of the mirror bright, and ever in position. It is to uncover the face which is to look at Christ, and draw down the veil when unhallowed sights are near. You have, perhaps, gone with an astronomer to watch him photograph the spectrum of a star. As you entered the dark vault of the Observatory you saw him begin by lighting a candle. To see the star with? No; but to see to adjust the instrument to see the star with. It was the star that was going to take the photograph; it was, also, the astronomer. For a long time he worked in the dimness, screwing tubes and polishing lenses and adjusting reflectors, and only after much labour the finely focussed instrument was brought to bear. Then he blew out the light, and left the star to do its work upon the plate alone. The day's task for the Christian is to bring his instrument to bear. Having done that he may blow out his candle. All the evidences of Christianity which have brought him there, all aids to Faith, all acts of Worship, all the leverages of the Church, all Prayer and Meditation, all girding of the Will—these lesser processes, these candle-light activities for that supreme hour may be set aside. But, remember, it is but for an hour. The wise man will be he who quickest lights his candle; the wisest he who never let it out. To-morrow, the next moment, he, a poor, darkened, slurred soul, may need it again to focus the Image better, to take a mote off the ens, to clear the mirror from a breath with which the world has dulled it.

No re-adjustment is ever required on behalf of the Star. That is one great fixed point in this shifting universe. But the world moves. And each day, each hour, demands a further motion and re-adjustment for the soul. A telescope in an observatory follows a star by clockwork, but the clockwork of the soul is called the Will. Hence, while the soul in passivity reflects the Image of the Lord, the Will in intense activity holds the mirror in position lest the drifting motion of the world bear it beyond the line of vision. To "follow Christ" is largely to keep the soul in such position as will allow for the motion of the earth. And this calculated counteracting of the movements of a world, this holding of the mirror exactly opposite to the Mirrored, this steadying of the faculties unerringly, through cloud and earthquake, fire and sword, is the stupendous co-operating labour of the Will. It is all man's work. It is all Christ's work. In practice, it is both; in theory it is both. But the wise man will say in practice, "It depends upon myself."

In the Galerie des Beaux Arts in Paris there stands a famous statue. It was the last work of a great genius, who, like many a genius, was very poor and lived in a garret which served as studio and sleeping-room alike. When the statue was all but finished, one midnight a sudden frost fell upon Paris. The sculptor lay awake in the fireless room and thought of the still moist clay, thought how the water would freeze in the pores and destroy in an hour the dream of his life. So the old man rose from his couch and heaped the bed-clothes reverently round his work. In the morning when the neighbours entered the room the sculptor was dead. But the statue lived.

The Image of Christ that is forming within us—that is life's one charge. Let every project stand aside for that "Till Christ be formed" no man's work is finished, no religion crowned, no life has fulfilled its end. Is the infinite task begun? When, how, are we to be different? Time cannot change men. Death cannot change men. Christ can. Wherefore, put on Christ.

12528713R00027

Made in the USA
Lexington, KY
18 December 2011